Saying Goodbye

Carmel Reilly
Cheryl Orsini

Australia • Brazil • Japan • Korea • Mexico • Singapore • Spain • United Kingdom • United States

Saying Goodbye

Fast Forward
Blue Level 11

Text: Carmel Reilly
Illustrations: Cheryl Orsini
Editor: Kate McGough
Design: Karen Mayo
Series design: James Lowe
Production controller: Emma Hayes
Audio recordings: Juliet Hill, Picture Start
Spoken by: Matthew King and Abbe Holmes
Reprint: Siew Han Ong

ISBN 978 0 17 012550 5
ISBN 978 0 17 012549 9 (set)

Cengage Learning Australia
Level 5 , 80 Dorcas Street
Southbank VIC 3006
Phone: 1300 790 853
Email: aust.nelsonprimary@cengage.com

For learning solutions, visit cengage.com.au

Printed in China by 1010 Printing International Ltd
8 9 10 26

This product is made from materials that are compliant with the EU Deforestation Regulation

Evaluated in independent research by staff from the Department of Language, Literacy and Arts Education at the University of Melbourne.

Saying Goodbye

Carmel Reilly
Cheryl Orsini

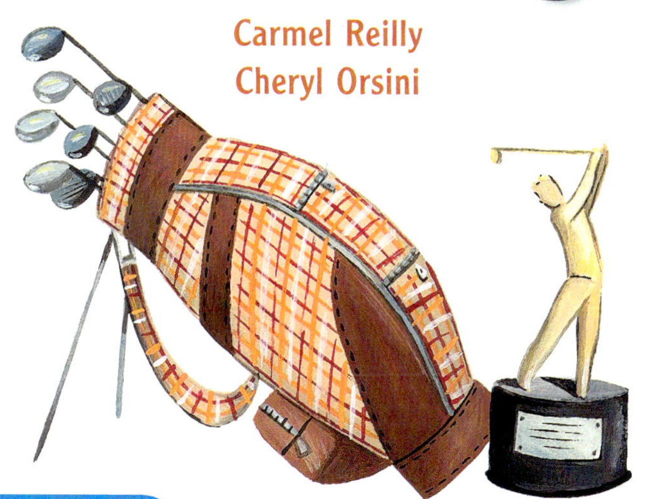

Contents

Getting Dressed Up

I feel really odd all dressed up.
Mum said I have to put on
my best clothes.
She said it's a big day today,
and we need to look good for Grandpa.

It's funny, because Grandpa never liked
getting dressed up much.
But Mum says that just for today
it's important.
So that's why I'm all dressed up.

Chapter 2

Remembering

I can't believe Grandpa is gone.
I keep thinking that he's going
to walk in here any time.

I can see him now.
His hair would stick up
on his head,
like ice-cream on top
of a cone.
I can see his brown skin,
all freckled from the sun.
I'll always remember his big smile.

Running Words 113

When Grandpa was a kid,
he was good at sport.
He got lots of prizes
for all kinds of things.

When he got older,
he started playing golf.
He also got lots of prizes for golf.

Running Words 150

After a while,
Grandma told Grandpa
he had to stop
playing golf.
She said there was no room left
in the house
for any of her things.
(But he didn't stop playing.)

Grandpa loved telling stories and jokes. He could even do magic tricks. Sometimes, he would find a coin behind one of my ears.

He would laugh
as he handed the coin to me.
His thin, freckled hand
would shake just a little.

Helping Out

Grandpa loved being in his garden. He liked to hear the radio when he worked.

Sometimes, I'd help him.
He would tell me funny stories
about when he was a boy.
Then I'd tell him all about school
and my friends.

Yesterday, Mum and I went over
to help Grandma.
For a little while, I didn't remember
that Grandpa had gone.
I went out into the garden
to look for him.

It was so quiet.
The radio wasn't on.
Suddenly, it hit me – I was never going
to see Grandpa again.

Saying Goodbye

Today, I am going to talk about Grandpa.
I will tell everyone about
what a good man he was.
I will tell them how much fun we had.
It's going to be hard
to say all these things,
but I think it will be good.
It will be a good way for me
to say goodbye.